D1518806

This book belongs to

Please
sign here...
_____

and here...
_____

and here.
_____

Fairy is a unicorn.

Now, that's not so strange.

But her powerful farts,

Please avoid at close range.

Her farts are a burst
of pink rainbow dust.
But run away fast,
if she lets one bust.

Most farts embarrass,
And make people blush.
But Fairy is proud,
And just farts when she must.

Some unicorns fly,
Though many cannot.
But when Fairy farts hard,
She takes off like a shot.

If someone's behind her, they'll be flattened for sure.

And be very lucky,
If they're not bruised
and sore.

Her farts are not stinky. They smell like spring flowers.

The scent is amazing.
It lingers for hours.

One day some bad poachers
Went deep into the forest.
They searched and hunted,
And would not give it a rest.

But Fairy was there to protect all her friends.
She knew about poachers and their evil ends.

She turned her back to them,
And lifted her tail.

She let a fart rip,
And the poachers turned tail.

They tried to escape,
But they had little chance.
They were blasted away,
And landed in France.

Fairy the Unicorns farts
Were used mostly for good.
And she tried to control them
Whenever she could.

If you saw a unicorn
High up in the sky,
You'd think it was Pegasus
With wings that could fly.

But Fairy is equipped
With jet propelled farts.
That let her take off
Like a rocket to Mars.

When she has to land,
She turns her bottom down.
Fairy releases tiny farts,
So she can float to the ground.

Fairy would fart like a blower.
And before very long,
Every unwanted leaf
Sang a goodbye song.

No other creature -
Furred, feathered, or horned,
Could fart with the skill
Of Fairy the Unicorn.

Her fart fame had spread
All over the world.
To the awe and excitement
Of all boys and girls.

Though their parents would scoff
And say, "Farting's not nice!"
If they had to fart,
They wouldn't think twice.

The children love Fairy
Wherever she goes.
But they make sure to test
Which way the wind blows.

Though her farts are fragrant,
they are still very strong.
And if you're in the 'blow zone',
you won't be there long.

Now Fairy's world famous,
that can't be denied.
And her farts can't be rivaled,
if anyone tried.

So the next time you see a unicorn in your town,
It may just be Fairy - the farter renowned.

Please go and greet her,
But stay away from her tail.
Her horn is much safer.
You won't be impaled.

To be continued...

Follow us on FB and IG @humorhealsus
To vote on new title names and freebies, visit us
at humorhealsus.com for more information.

@humorhealsus

@humorhealsus

CPSIA information can be obtained
at www.ICGtesting.com
Printed in the USA
BVHW020221261022
650235BV00010B/616